IT'S ALL ABOUT THE HAT

Poems about Famous Paintings and Artists

LUCY ANN LINNEY

KDP

Copyright © 2020 Lucy Ann Linney

All rights reserved

No part of this book may be reproduced, or stored in a retrieval system, or transmitted in any form or by any means, electronic, mechanical, photocopying, recording, or otherwise, without express written permission of the publisher.

ISBN-13: 9798683098971

*First of all dedicated to the memory of my sister June, the bravest beauty.
Also dedicated to my talented sisters Pam and Angela for their artistic inspiration.
To my husband David and children Jim, Hannah and Sarah for believing in me.
To my brother and wondeful family for their support.*

"I love Brittany. I find wildness and primitiveness there. When my wooden clogs ring on the granite, I hear the muffled, dull and powerful tone which I try to bring to my painting."

PAUL GAUGUIN

CONTENTS

Title Page	1
Copyright	2
Dedication	3
Epigraph	4
Introduction	7
IT'S ALL ABOUT THE HAT	9
LISA DEL GIOCONDO	12
THE FIGHTING TEMERAIRE	16
BOIS DE BOULOGNE	19
DON'T GET THE WRONG IMPRESSION	22
MONET'S GARDEN	25
MY LITTLE DAISY FRIEND	27
IS THIS MY FAVOURITE PAINTING?	30
HARVEST FEST	33
DID THE EYE JUST WINK?	36
AN ARMY OF SUNFLOWERS	39
STOLEN	42
TO HEAR TO SEE TO FEEL	48
Acknowledgement	53
About The Author	55
Books By This Author	57

INTRODUCTION

My family has been hugely inflential in shaping whom I have become.
My mother was a gifted pianist and played the church organ; my dad was a singer and campanologist.
As a family, we have been called the Von Trapps on more than one occasion.
Weekends were taken up with church attendance, bellringing and choir. So as a girl I became aware of tones, harmonies and melody.
My sisters could paint too. Pam drew sketches in "Mabel Lucie Attwell style" and once decorated the school common room wall with coloured horses in impressionistic style. She also also painted scenary for the local Operatic and Dramatic society.
Angels's talent blossomed later and she exhibits her work locally.
Surrounded by painters, singers and campanology, why I am I writing a poetry book?

Every year my husband and I go to our holiday home in the south west of France, to an area called The Gers, where sunflowers bloom and rolling hills stretch as far as the eye can see.
There was no television or computer at the beginning, so we both began to write. I wrote my first poem and David said. "I like that."
That was all the encouragement I needed.

IT'S ALL ABOUT THE HAT

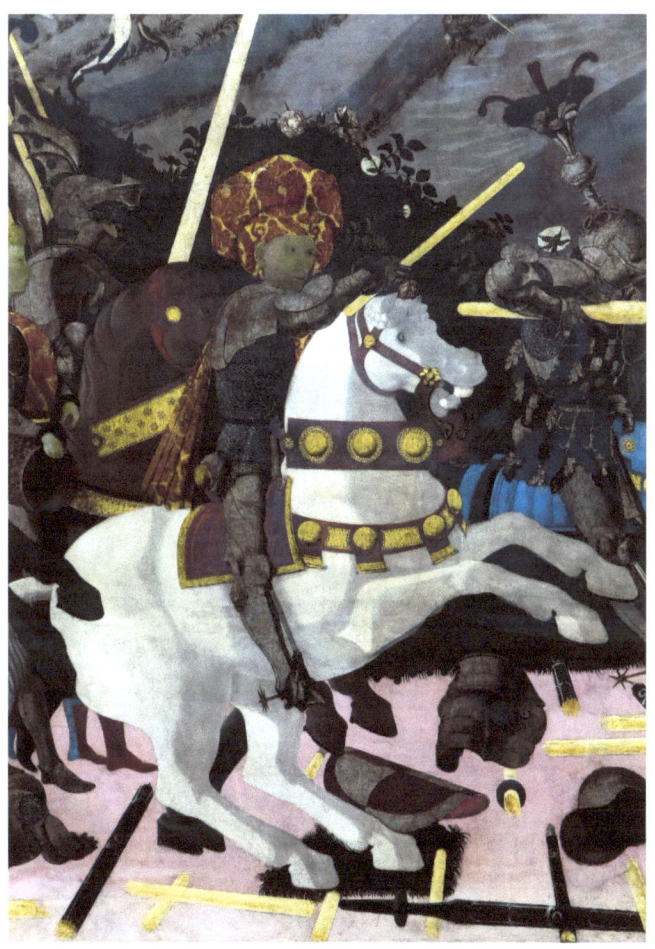

"Courage above all things is the first quality of a warrior."
Karl Van Clausewitz

It's all about the hat,
decorated red and gold,
on the head of Tolentino,
the reckless brave and bold.
The colour, shape and size
of the onion dome creation,
instead of a soldier's helmet
is the focus of narration.
The Italian condottiere is
the hero of this drama,
played out in technicolor
with background panorama.
On charger white, he leads his men
with deadly lance held steady;
massing troops do crowd the field
for conflict they are ready.
Elements of gold and silver
shimmer, shine and glint
on cavalcaded armour,
highly polished, newly mint.
The lances on the ground,
were angled in a way
to give linear perspective
while the backdrop fades away.
The San Romano conflict
back in fourteen thirty two,
found Florence fighting Siena;
skirmishes were nothing new.
But, the hat takes centre stage,
telling its distinctive story,
symbolic of leadership,
status, power and glory.

Painting: - The Battle of San Romano 1432

Artist: - Paolo Uccello 1397 - 1475

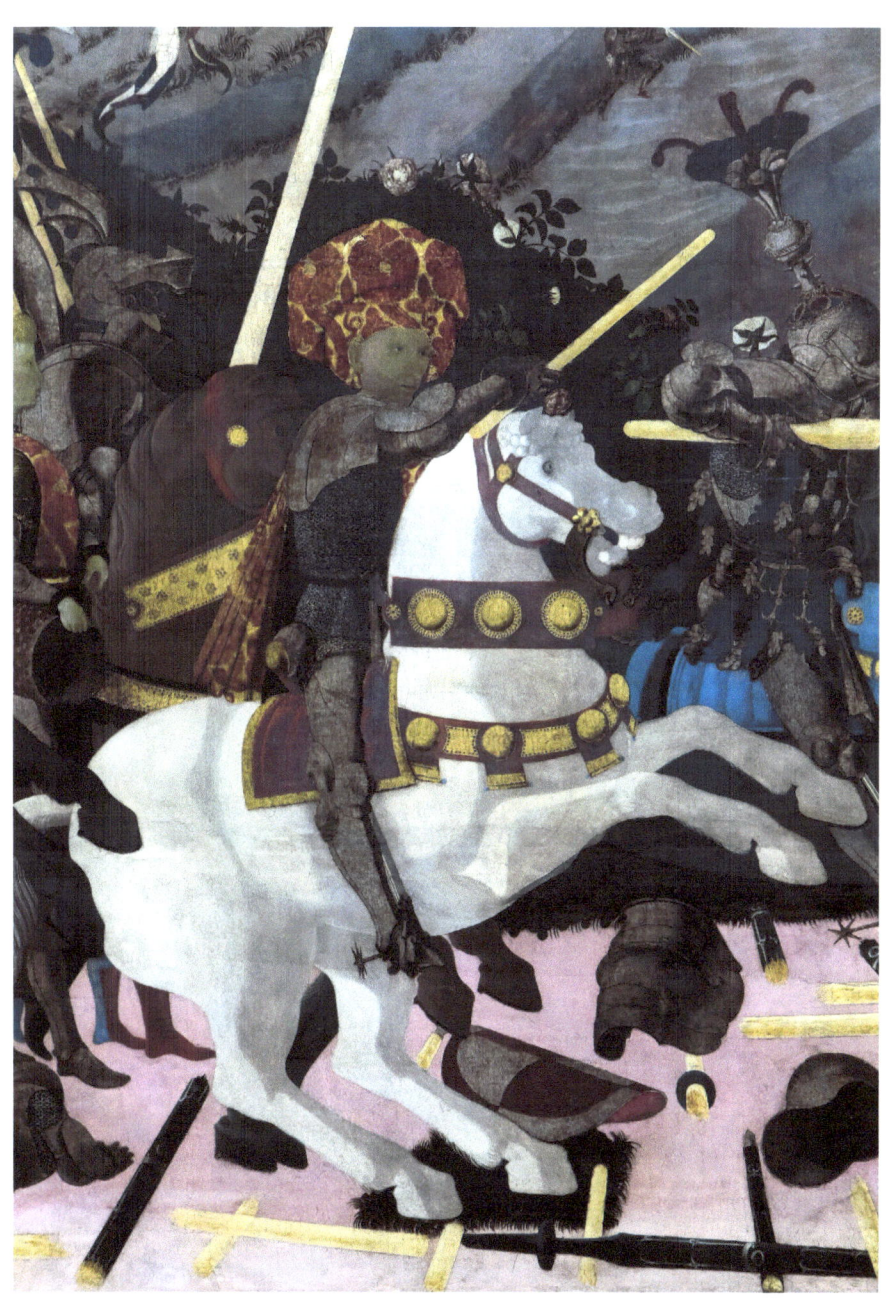

LISA DEL GIOCONDO

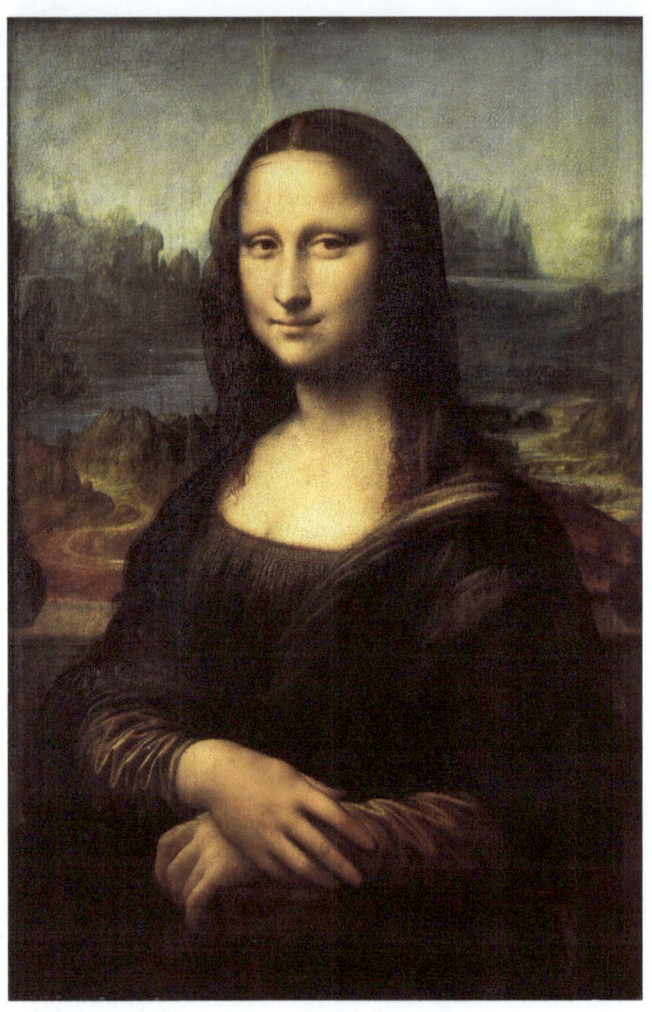

"Mona Lisa is the only beauty who went through history and retained her reputation." Will Rogers

Lisa del Giocondo
was born in Italy.
Leonardo caught her essence
in the fifteen century.
Her portrait hung in stately rooms
of Francis the French king
at Fontainbleau
with decor of exquisite colouring.
A possession highly prized
at Louis's palace of Versailles;
two centuries of patronage
safe passage would imply.
But no! Her frame discarded
like forsaken cast off lover,
Napoleon to the rescue,
her background did discover.
Her authenticity, an emblem
added to his spoils,
reminiscent of Our Lady,
beatified in oils.
Her fame continued on
it's course a veritable tease,
to Europe and beyond,
like Chinese whispers on the breeze.
Mon Dieu! Stolen!
No simple by your leave?
Purloined, taken to Florence,

leaving Paris folks to grieve?
The space left by her passing
was both vacuous and small,
a nation thus awakened
came to view the empty wall.
The patriotic thief
was dealt with rather leniently,
whilst back inside the Louvre
her ranking grew appreciably.
Venerated status
to her was thus afforded,
five hundred years of patronage
was finally rewarded.
Transported far beyond the realms
of mortal works of art.
She is part of our psyche,
Madonna of our heart.

◆ ◆ ◆

Painting: - Mona Lisa
Lisa Del Giocondo 1503

Artist: - Leonardo Da Vinci
1452 - 1519

The Mona Lisa painting was stolen in 1911, when a handyman working in the Louvre, took it off the wall and hid it under a smock.
With the smock and the painting under his arm, he calmly walked out of the building. He took it back to Florence, thinking that he would be celebrated as a hero. The painting was returned to the Louvre in 1913.

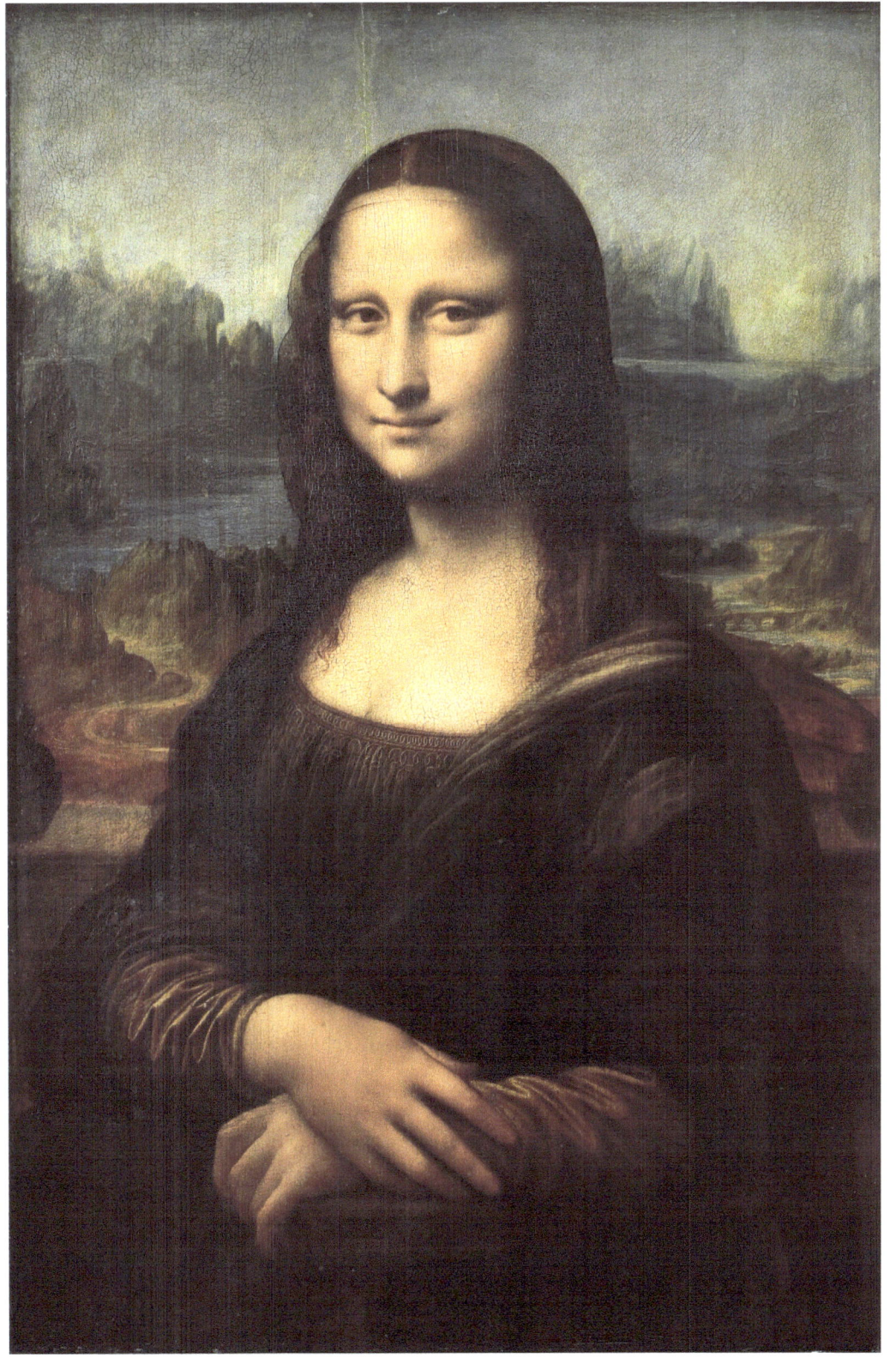

THE FIGHTING TEMERAIRE

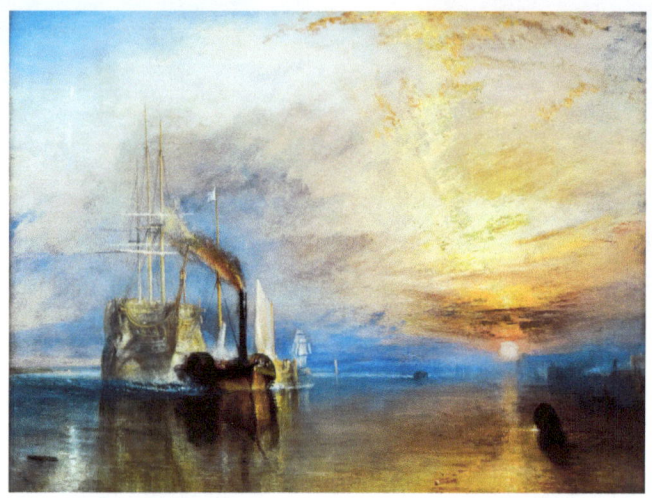

"England expects that every man will do his duty." Horatio Nelson

Coursing through waves in full sail,
naval ships under Nelson's command.
Two vertical queues
face an enemy line,
a sea faring strategy planned.

Nipping the heels of the flagship,
Temeraire is told to stay back.
Nelson's columns draw near
to Trafalgar,
English fleet is set to attack.

Temeraire picks a fight with a
Spanish beast of a ship, four decks high.
Black smoke billows forth,
thick and acrid.
Chaos! Surprise! Then a cry!

The French flagship targets Nelson.
The Victory is damaged, in trouble.
No time for doubt,
Temeraire brought about
and rams the French ship at the double.

A pole falls atop Temeraire,
it's men run across the mainmast.
Hard fighting ensues,
two formIdable crews,
but the French must surrender at last.

The Fougneux is blasted with shot,
as it tried in vain, to surprise.
Now three ships
are all lashed together;
Temeraire sails to port with her prize.

How can it be tugged off for scrap?
Turner hit an emotional chord,
when he painted the heart breaking end
of the warship the nation adored.

◆ ◆ ◆

"Indistinction is my forte." J. M. W. Turner

Painting: -The Fighting Temeraire

Artist: -J. M. W. Turner 1775 -1839

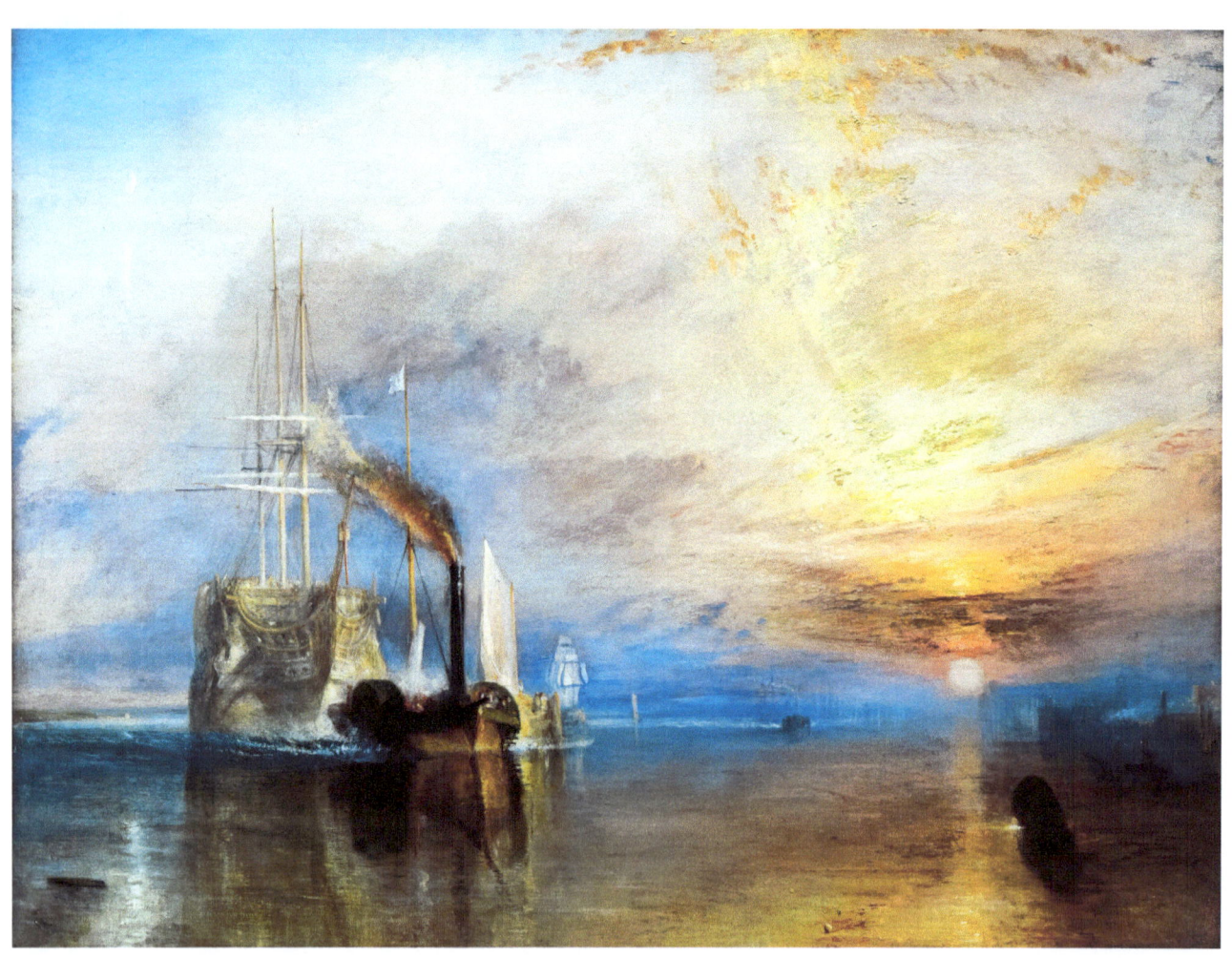

BOIS DE BOULOGNE

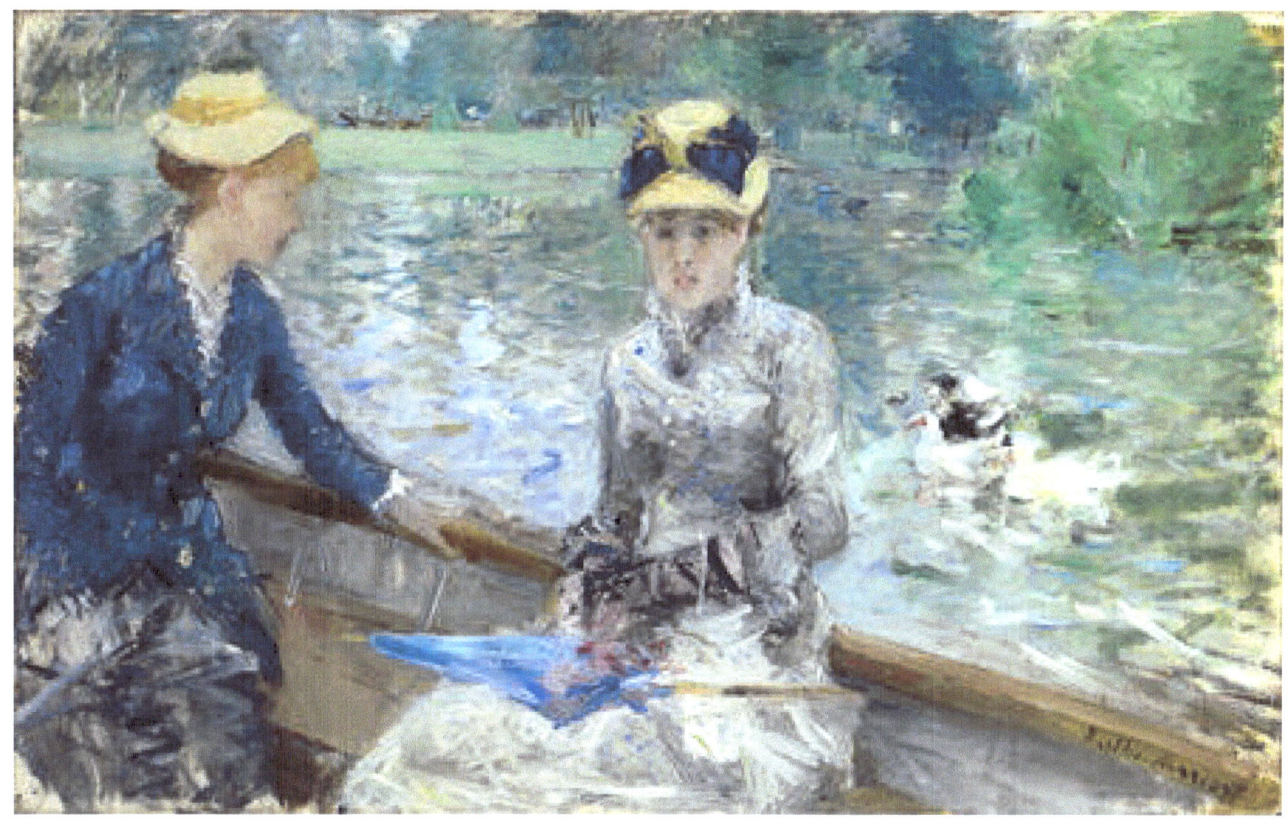

"My ambition is limited to capturing something intransient." Berthe Morisot

An artist, a woman, a French lady,
Berthe Morisot was part
of the Bourgeoisie.
Educated, connected with Paris greats,
Renoir and Manet were associates.

Intelligent, articulate,
an impressionist,
worked at the Louvre as a copyist.
Underrated, pioneering flair,
enjoyed outdoor painting -en plein air.

Colours yellow, blue and green,
her palette in this lakeside scene.
Zigzag brushwork, shimmering light,
a virtuoso in shades of white.

Summer's Day sees ladies in a boat,
pretty hats and smart blue coat,
umbrella prop, theatrical set,
Rococo influence, tete a tete.

Painted homely gentle folk
adding features with one stroke.
The sitter, faltering expression,
hints at feminine oppression.

Subject to artist, eye connecton
taking art in a new direction.
Critiqued unjustly for domestic style,
Morisot prevailed with a truthful smile.

◆ ◆ ◆

Berthe Morisot was a painter full of eighteenth century delicacy and grace, in a word, the last elegant and feminine artist since Fragonard." Pierre Auguste Renoir

Painting: - Summer's Day

Artist: - Berthe Morisot 1841 - 1895

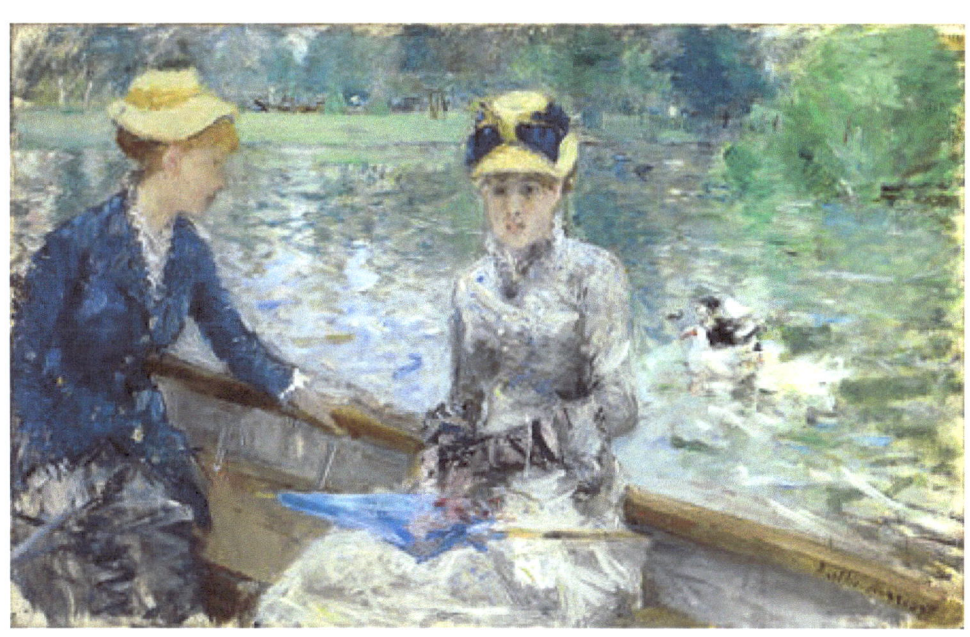

DON'T GET THE WRONG IMPRESSION

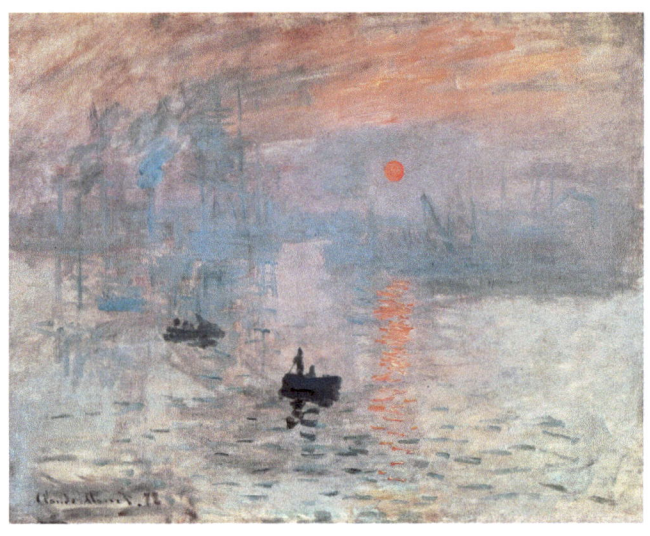

" I will do water, beautiful blue water." - Claude Monet

Remember those men from the past,
whose notions left us aghast?
Such passionate guys
which was no surprise,
anti - authority they would be classed.

In secret the sect rallied round,
a like minded club they did found.
Full of intrigue,
this elaborate league
met in cafes and bars underground.

"Oh dear, it's a total disaster!"
commented one critical master.
"Your lines are obscured
and the detail is flawed,
an impression is not what we're after."

"Impression! That's it." Monet cried,
with Renoir and pals at his side.
"Our brush strokes are thin,
but that's how we'll win;
let colour and light be our guide."

America loved all their art.
Sales soared right off the chart;
while fresh landscape scenes
and intimate themes
made the impressionist clique stand apart.

Usher in a new art episode
Realism and truth as it's code.
What the artists saw
was right at the core
and the rule book was seen to explode.

The Impressionist Clique included:
 Claude Monet, Pierre Auguste Renoir, Alfred Sisley, Paul Cezanne, Camille Pissarro, Edgar Degas, Berthe Morisot and Eugene Boudin

Painting: - Le Havre - Impression Sunrise 1874

Artist: - Claude Monet 1840 - 1926

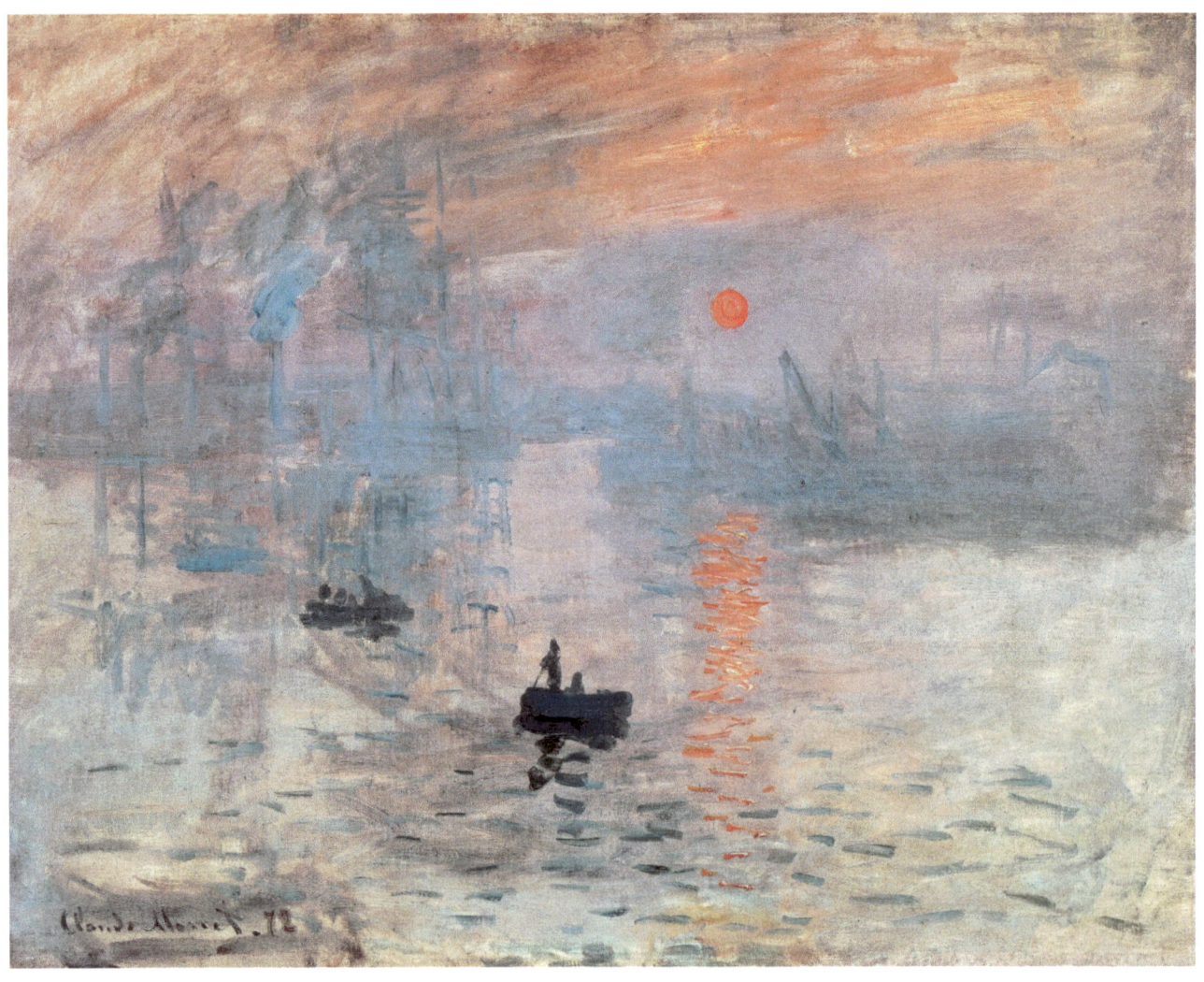

MONET'S GARDEN

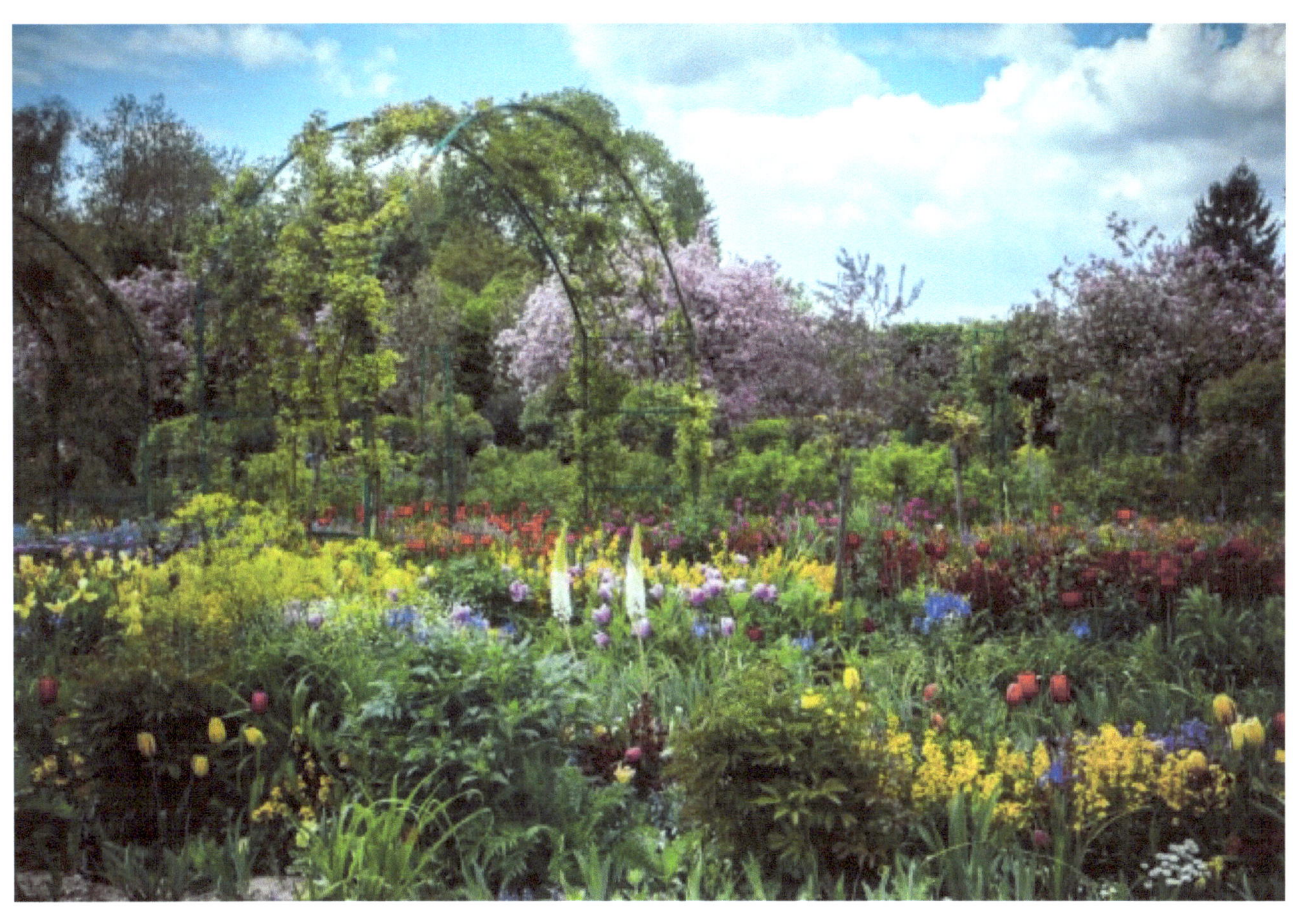

"My garden is my most beautiful masterpiece." Claude Monet

He loved his exquisite garden,
bright flowers on showy display,
perpetuating a painter's palette
set out in vivid array.
Busy lizzies, geraniums, zinneas,
lilies and plants from abroad
fashioned a riot of colour
in the French home he adored.

Eight gardeners maintained this beauty;
what a place to create, what a sight.
He painted the world as he saw it
in many stages of light.
The powers that be at the Louvre
regarded his paintings at last.
To be a great painter and gardener
was surely all one man could ask.

◆ ◆ ◆

Photo: - The Artist's Garden at Giverny

Claude Monet 1840 - 1926

MY LITTLE DAISY FRIEND

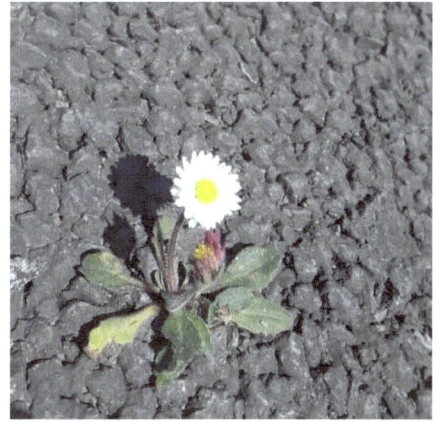

My daughter Sarah, who lives in France, found this daisy growing in the lane by her house. I wrote a poem about it and have included it next to Monet's garden.

I didn't expect to see you there
on the cold rough tarmac road.
No soil around to bed you in,
no green grass, freshly mowed.
You're stalwart and you don't give up,
you're here, there, everywhere,
except in the antarctic
with it's frozen hostile air.

I didn't expect to see you there,
being where you're not meant.
As cool as someone in a bar,
they often do frequent.
Completely innocent and unaware of any sin,
eyes open at one hint of dawn,
thus does your day begin.

I didn't expect to see you there,
my little daisy friend,
your power of healing wrapped up
in that white and yellow blend.
Razzmatazz and party
with bees and insects, but
only until night fall,
when your petals softly shut.

◆ ◆ ◆

Photo of a daisy
By Sarah Oakey Kirkwood

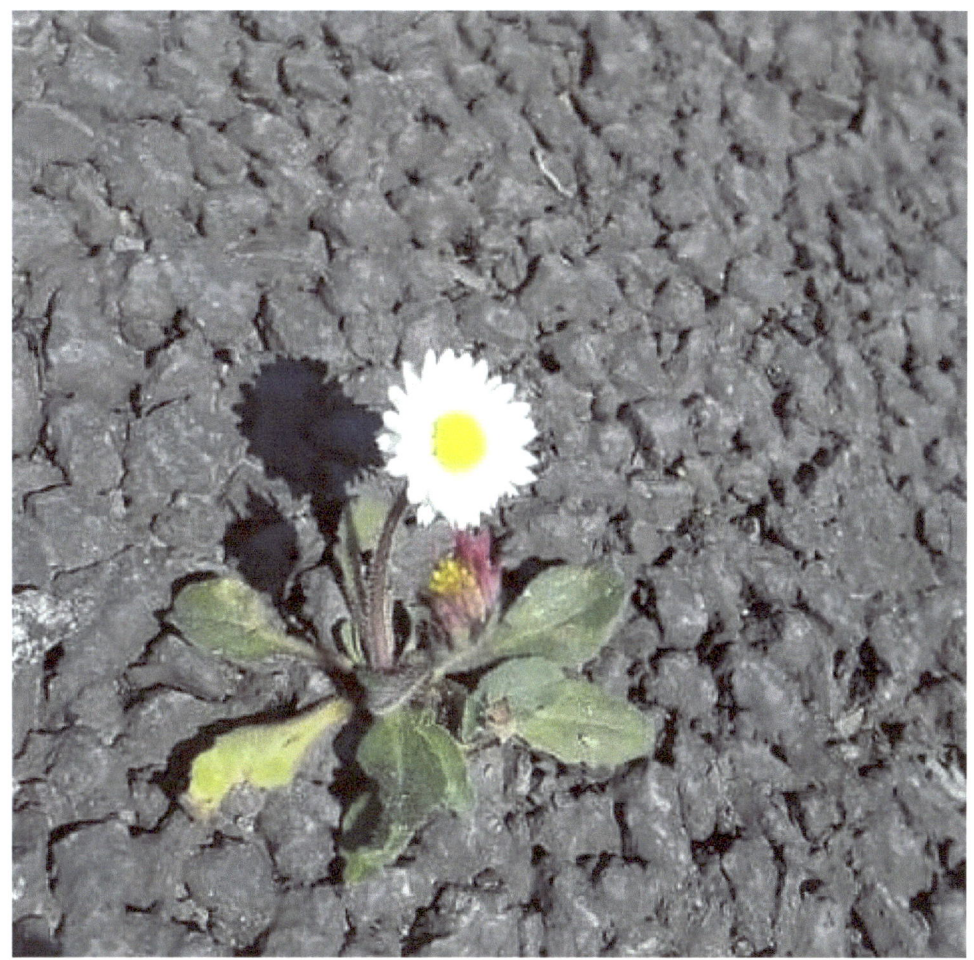

IS THIS MY FAVOURITE PAINTING?

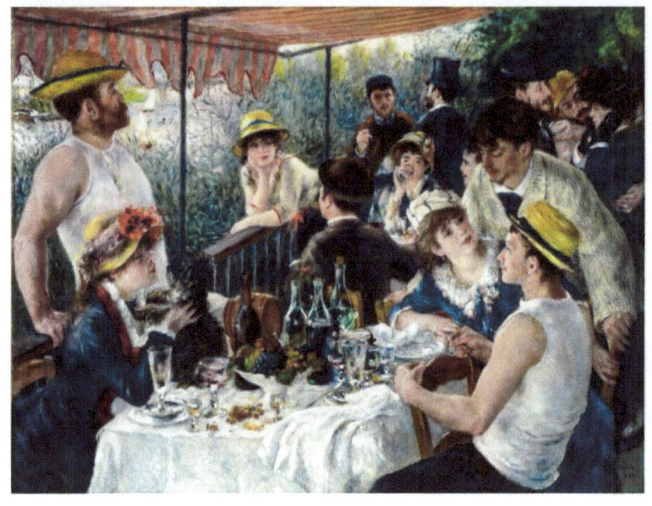

"Why shouldn't art be pretty? There are enough unpleasant things in the world." Pierre Auguste Renoir

Is this my favourite painting?
It surely has to be
the one that deeply resonates
with life's rich tapestry.

Renoir caught the easy going

atmosphere of fun,
with impressionistic background
back in eighteen eighty one.

His skill, beyond exemption
taking beauty to new heights,
clever use of vibrant colour
conjured gladness in his sights.

Romance is on the canvas
crystal clear for all to see;
body language speaks of love
and simple joie de vie.

Imagine being party to that
luncheon symphony,
extemporising banter
in illustrious company!

But did you know he suffered
from acute arthritic pain?
You wouldn't know from looking
at his painting on the Seine.

Negativity was hidden
out of mind and sight,
instead for everyone to see
was charm and pure delight.

"One morning, one of us ran out of black, it was the birth of impressionism." Pierre Auguste Renoir

Painting: - Luncheon of the Boating Party 1881

Artist - Pierre Auguste Renoir 1841 - 1919

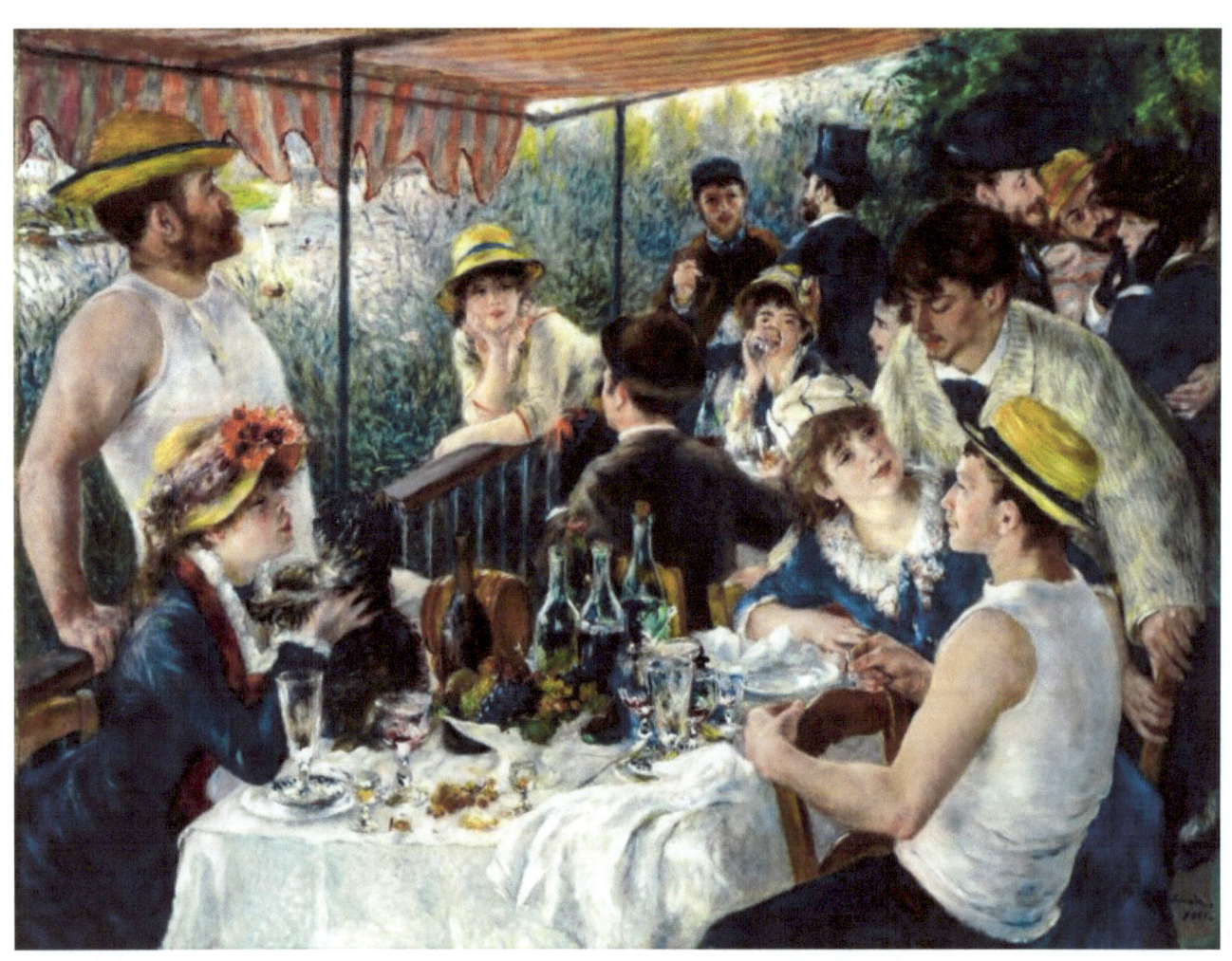

HARVEST FEST

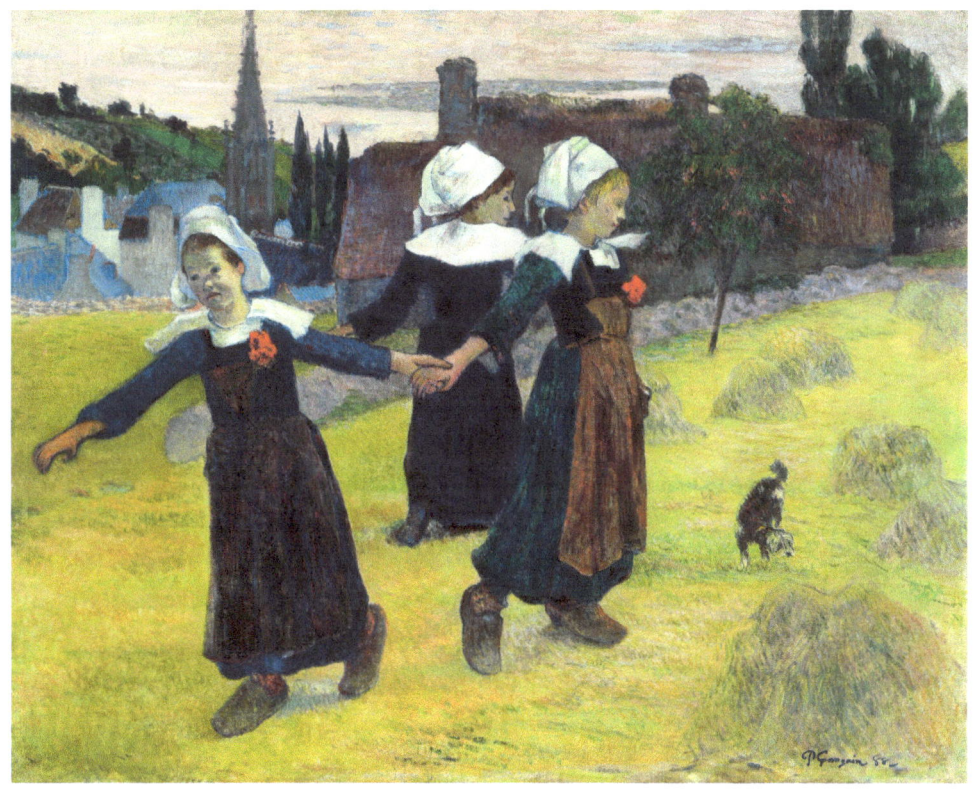

"Art is not what you see, but what you make others see." Paul Gauguin

The dog is given a wistful glance
as the Breton girls step to the beat,
concentration on their faces,
wooden sabots upon their feet.

Celtic past forever present
celebrating Harvest Fest.
Statement rose and lacy bonnets
adorn the girls in Sunday best.

Gauguin loved the local colour,
roofs of houses, trees and woods.
He painted the authentic dress of ladies
in their crisp, white hoods.

Capturing the rural flavour
in paintings that he worked upon,
Gauguin found a peaceful haven
with his ilk in Pont Aven.

◆ ◆ ◆

Painting: - Breton Girls Dancing 1883

Artist: - Paul Gauguin 1848 - 1903

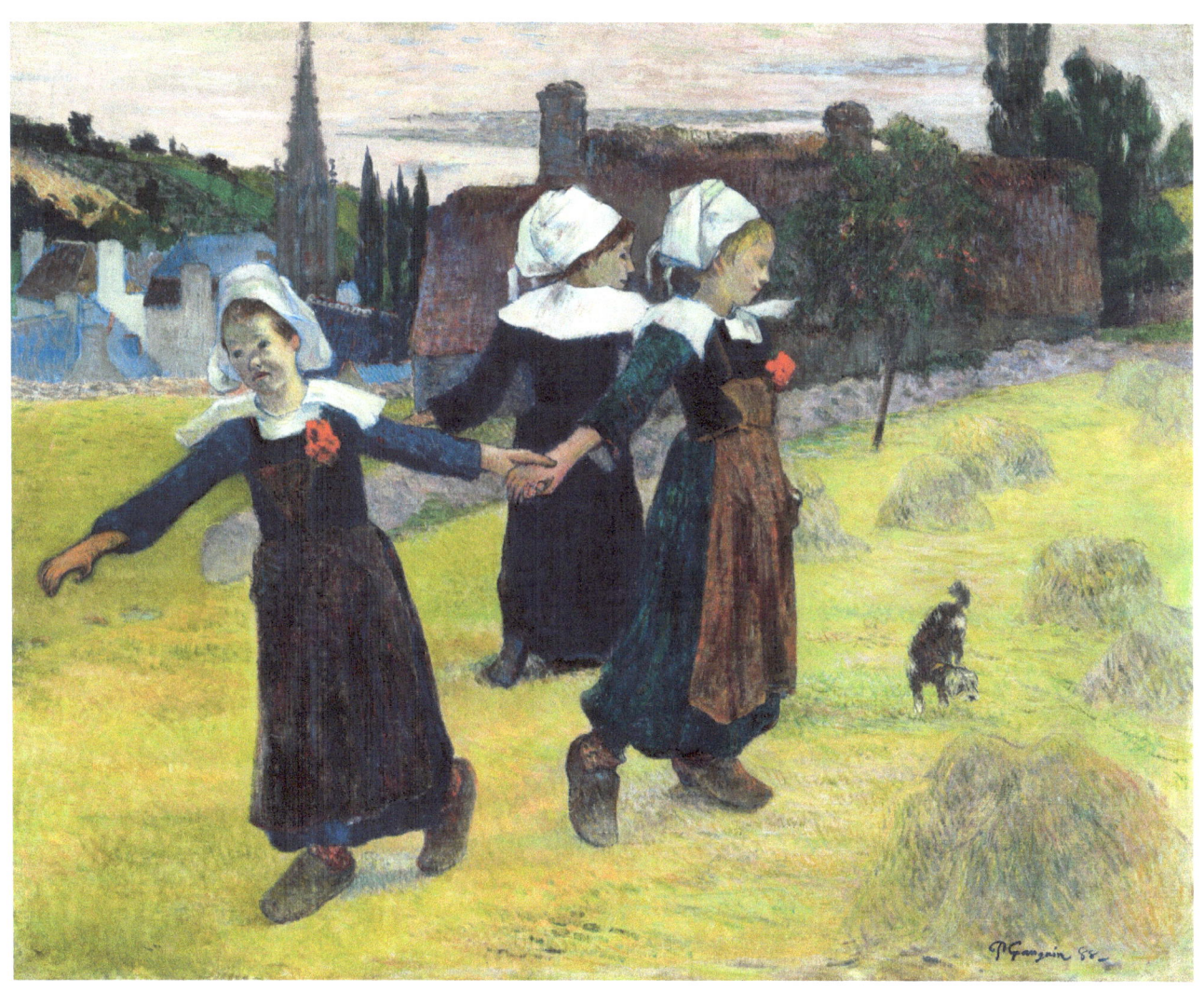

DID THE EYE JUST WINK?

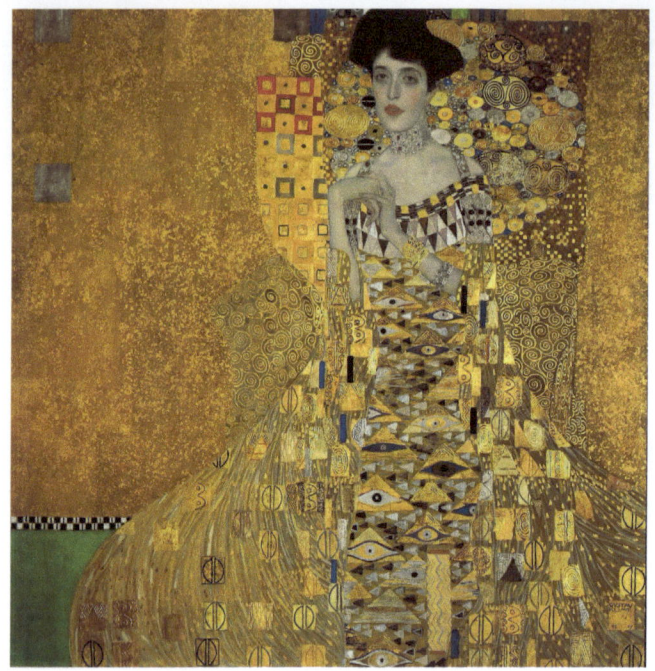

"Outer beauty attracts, but inner beauty captivates." Kate Angell

Did the eye just wink?
Am I party to this painting's soul?
Bewitching like a peacock's tail,
eyes attract; was that Klimt's goal?

Egyptian eyes of silver and black,
triangular eyelids ornately gold.
A variegated mix of glittering shapes,
refract and reflect in metal, cold.

Armour ready to hide or shield,
no gaps or chinks in this
garnished lace.
Camouflage in open view shouts,
"Keep your distance! Know your place."

In a gilded cage, is she snared
like the emperor's tuneful nightingale?
Bespangled choker, ribbon chain
frames the face with the skin so pale.

Jewels, silverleaf, bells and coins,
the trappings of wealth gleaming bright,
will never engulf the pure majesty
of the lady immersed in the light.

Painting: - Lady in Gold Adele Bloch Bauer 1907

Artist: - Gustav Klimt 1862 - 1913

LUCY ANN LINNEY

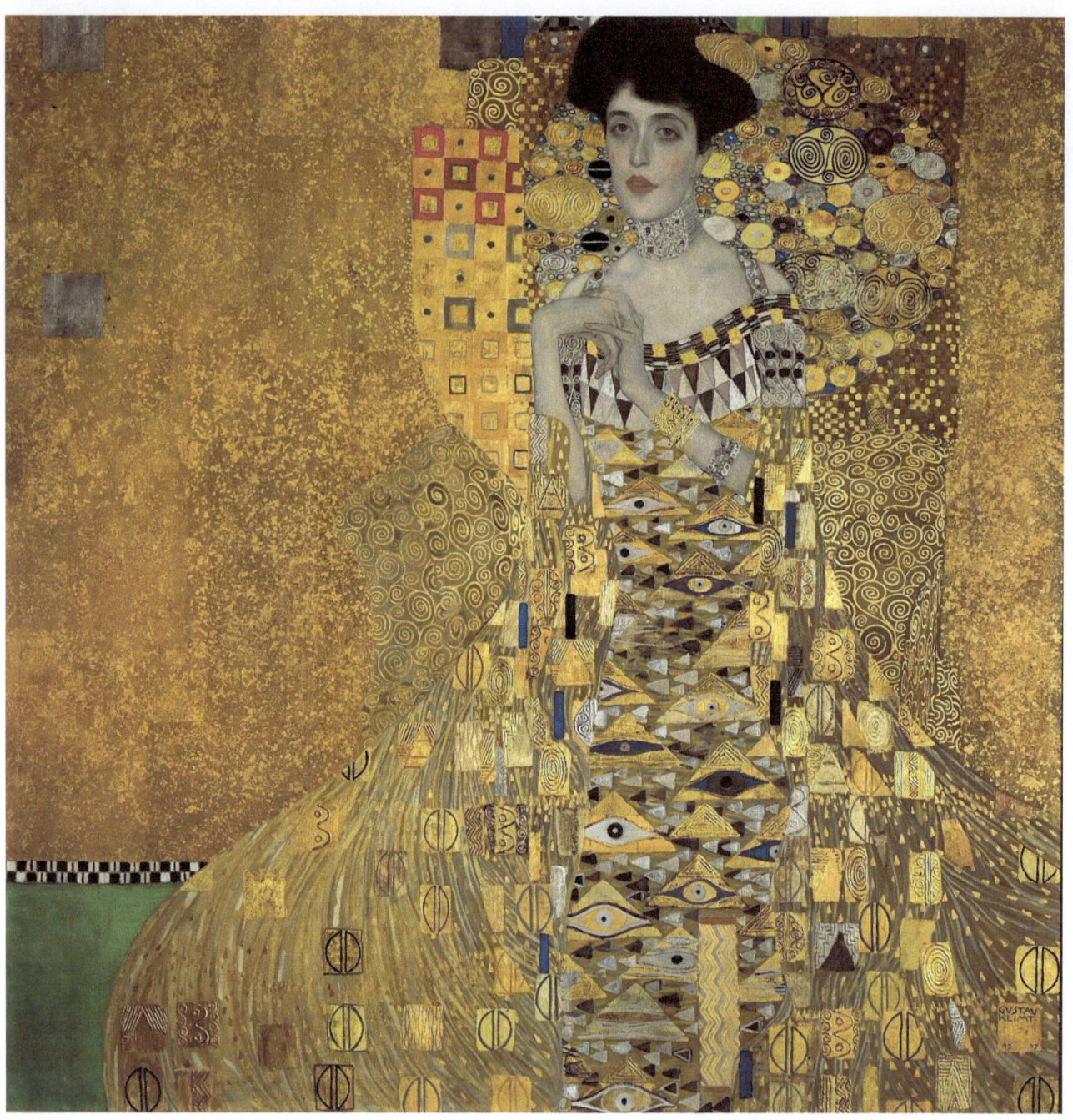

AN ARMY OF SUNFLOWERS

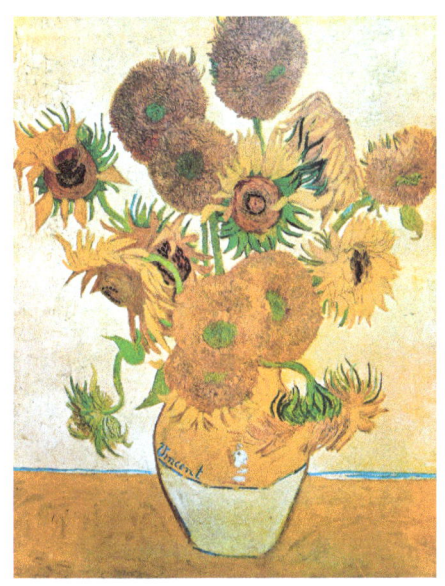

"Keep your face to the sun and you cannot see the shadow. It's what sunflowers do." Helen Keller

Awe inspiring
statuesque flower,
regarding the sunshine
hour by hour.
Heads turn en masse,
instructions not given,
total compliance

by the sun driven.
Bright yellow petals,
black central spot
viewed at a distance
reduced to a dot.
Counterpane covering,
field after field,
developing ripeness
their oil to yield.
Uniformed army
resplendent in gold,
passive they stand,
their ranks extolled.
Icarus like
are they aiming too high?
Counterfeit soldiers
it's time to say bye.
Autumn moves on
and gold turns to brown,
glory has faded,
defences are down.
Battalions of combines!
The sunflowers pall,
defeated and headless,
a warning to all.
An artist was spellbound;
Vincent by name,

sunflowers did paint
at the height of his fame.

◆ ◆ ◆

Painting: - Sunflowers 1888

**Artist: - Vincent Van Gogh
1853 - 1890**

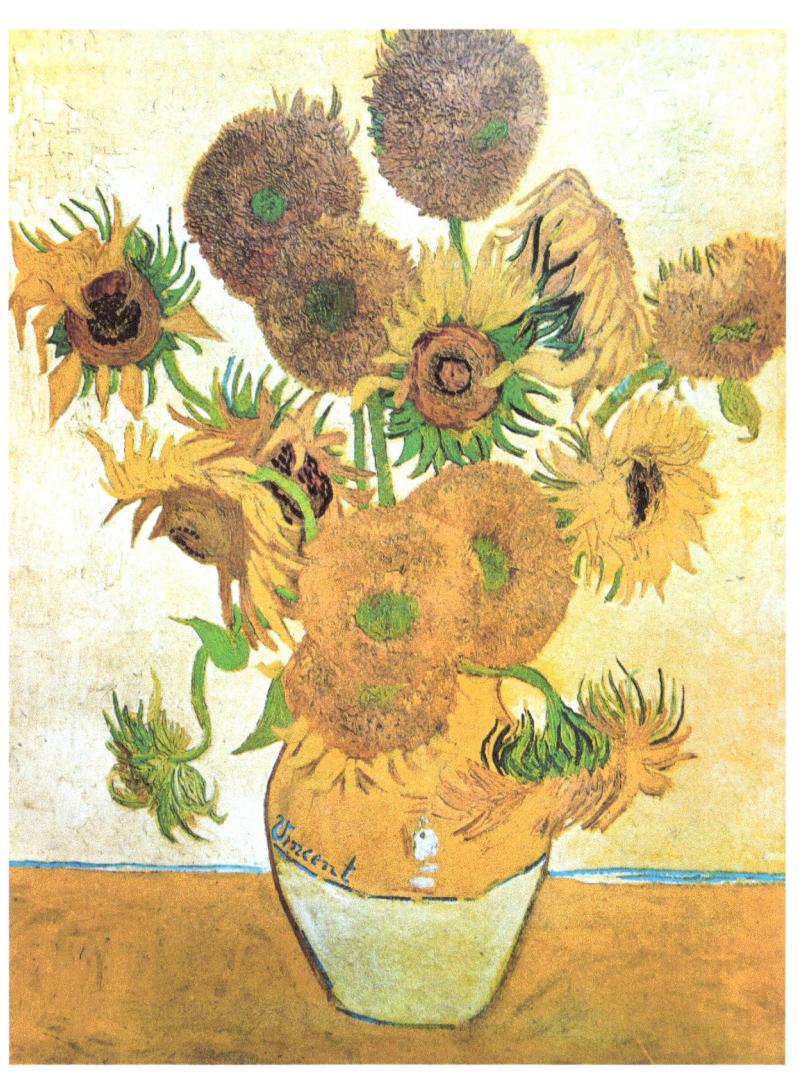

STOLEN

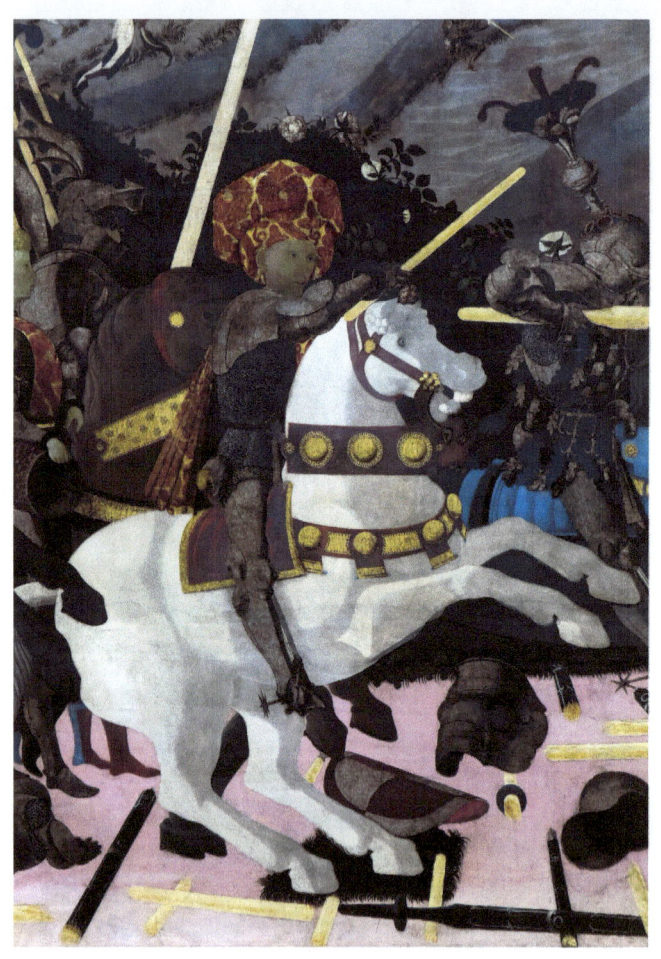

The Battle Of San Romano

Lorenzo de Medici
clapped eyes upon the hat,
the hat of red and gold, he said
"I'd like to purchase that."
But there were two more paintings
in Uccello's triptych set.
Lorenzo took them too
without remorse, without regret.
Each panel, three foot long
was based on gothic, window style.
Lorenzo cut the tops right off,
that vandal, full of guile.
The Bartilini brothers tried
their birthright to reclaim,
but to the patron of the arts,
all this was just a game.
In the Medici palace
did he sit and contemplate
on the San Romano battle
that Uccello did create?
The final resting places
of the triptych, so desired
are Florence, London, Paris -
individually admired.

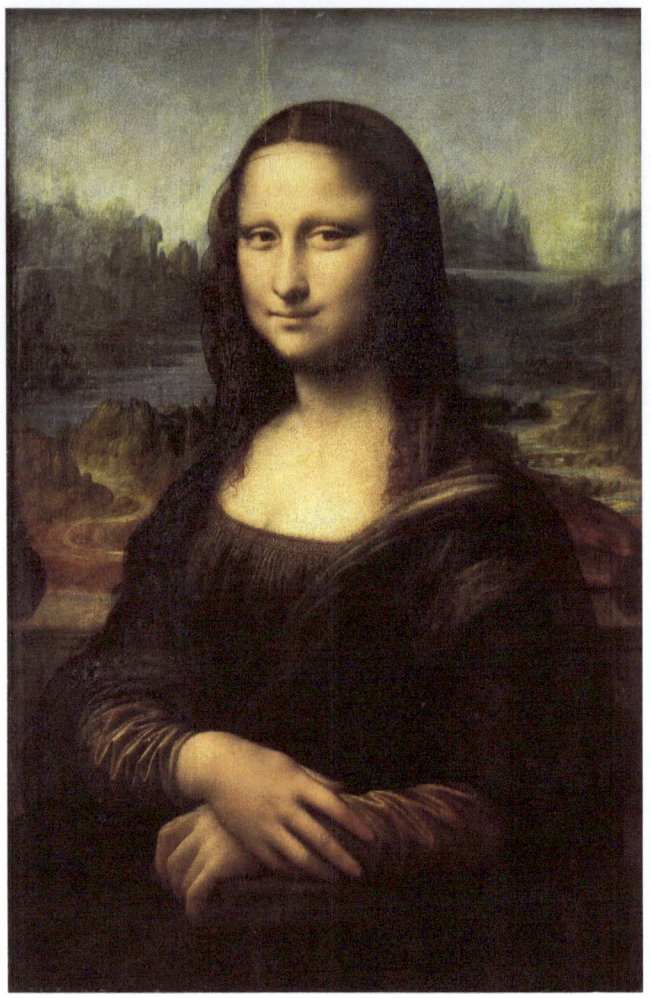

Mona Lisa

More art works have been stolen
than I would like to mention.
A handyman went in the Louvre
and stole without detection.

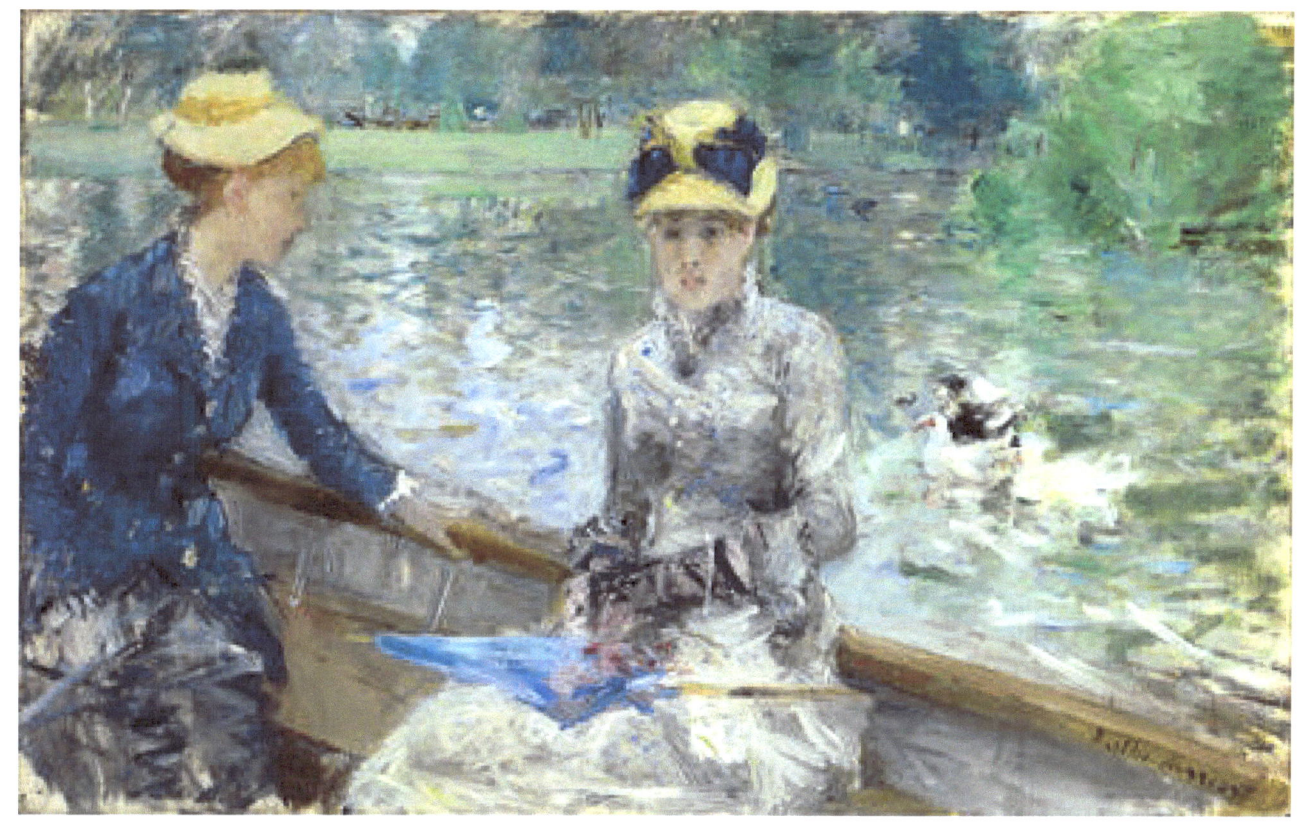

Summer's Day

Summer's Day was stolen
back in nineteen fifty eight,
by two disgruntled students
when they visited the Tate.
"This should be in Ireland as
bequested by Hugh Lane.
Just to let 'em know
it's Dublin's loss and London's gain."

LUCY ANN LINNEY

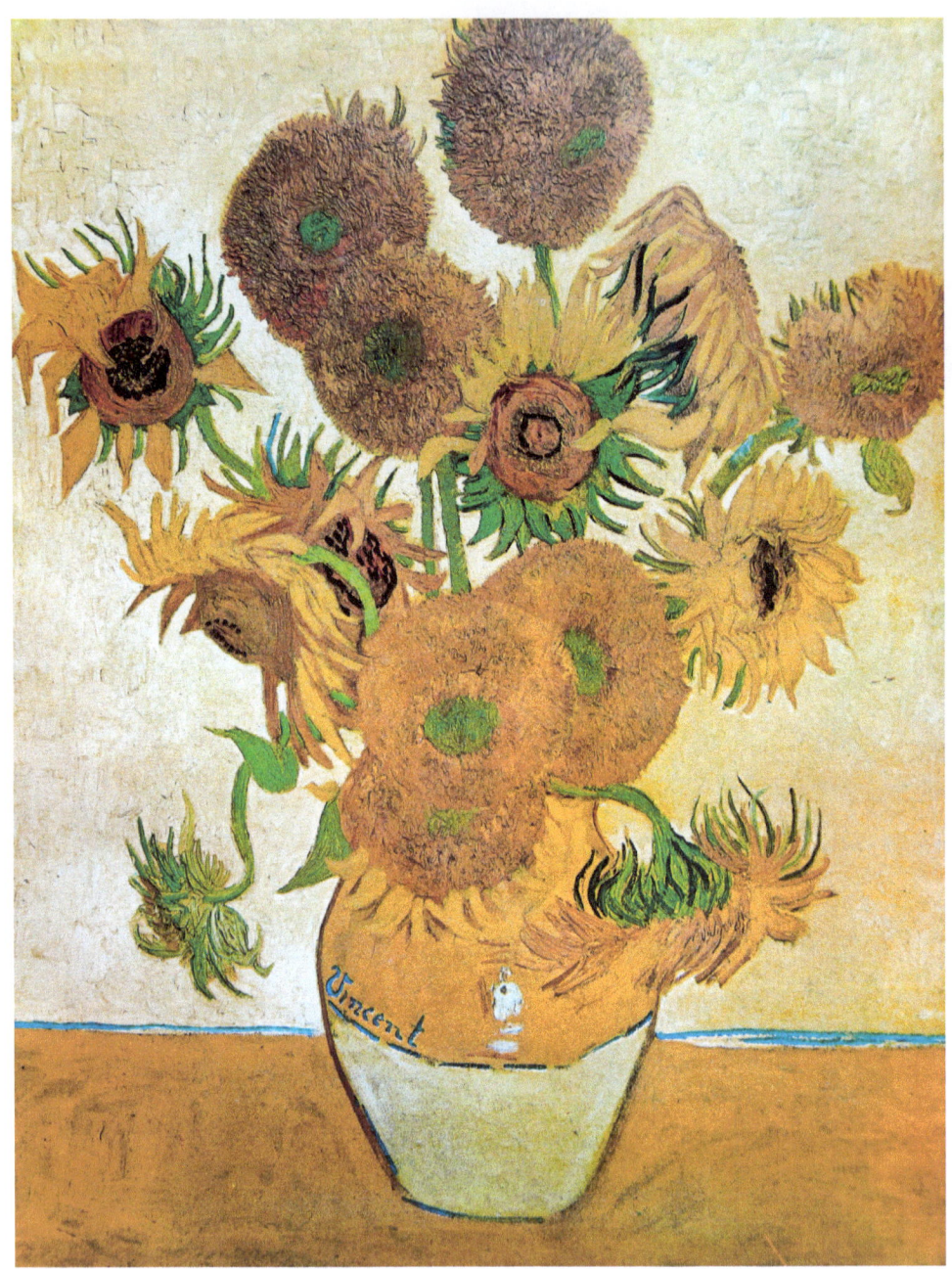

Sunflowers

This work of art was stolen
but it didn't go too far,
along with other paintings
found abandoned in a car.

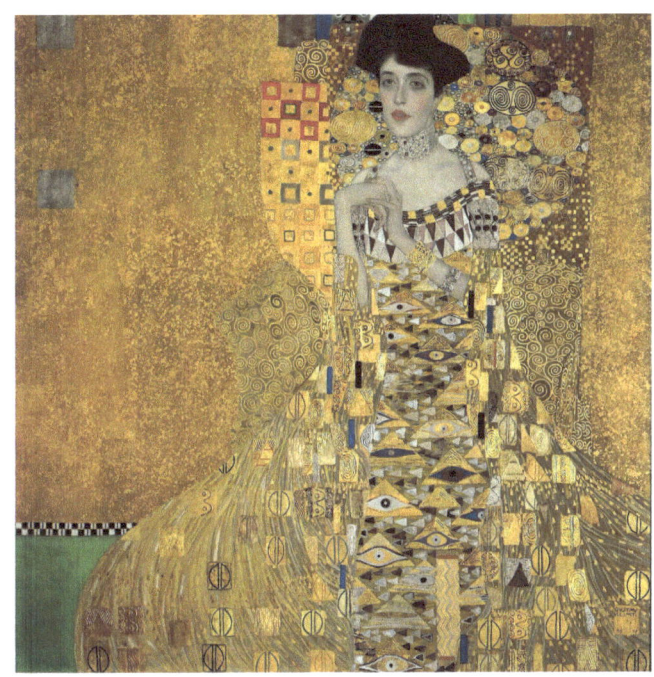

Lady In Gold

A casualty of war.
A war of dominance and theft,
cruelty and greed
leaving families bereft.
The weak had to succumb to men
purporting to be strong,
but they were weak,
disfunctional and absolutely wrong.
The Lady was returned
because the neice would not give in.
The culprits left with nothing,
giving decency the win.

TO HEAR TO SEE TO FEEL

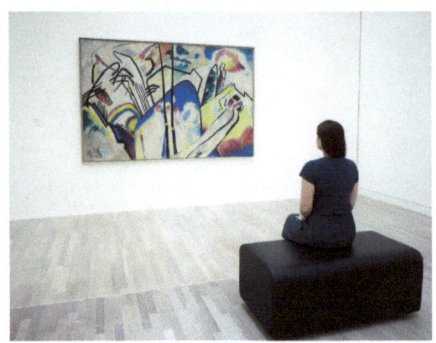

" Art, especially music exists to elevate us as far as possible
above everyday existence." Gabriel Faure

I wonder what Kandinsky heard,
I wonder what he saw?
Did he feel like the composer
of a vast orchestral score?

Faure composed a requiem,
a masterpiece of art,
eliciting emotion
and tugging at the heart.

Latin posed no barriers
for the listener's connection.
Chords in tonal sequence;
Faure made a great selection.

We don't need to know
if they were 7ths, 5ths or 3rds;
our souls just like the feeling
without the need for words.

High angelic voices
soar up to the heights above,
singing out the melody
that speaks of joy and love.

A glorious crescendo
with layering of sound,
as minor follows major
in this eulogy profound.

But, now back to Kandinsky
tell us is there just a chance,
we can listen to your colours
and follow in your dance?

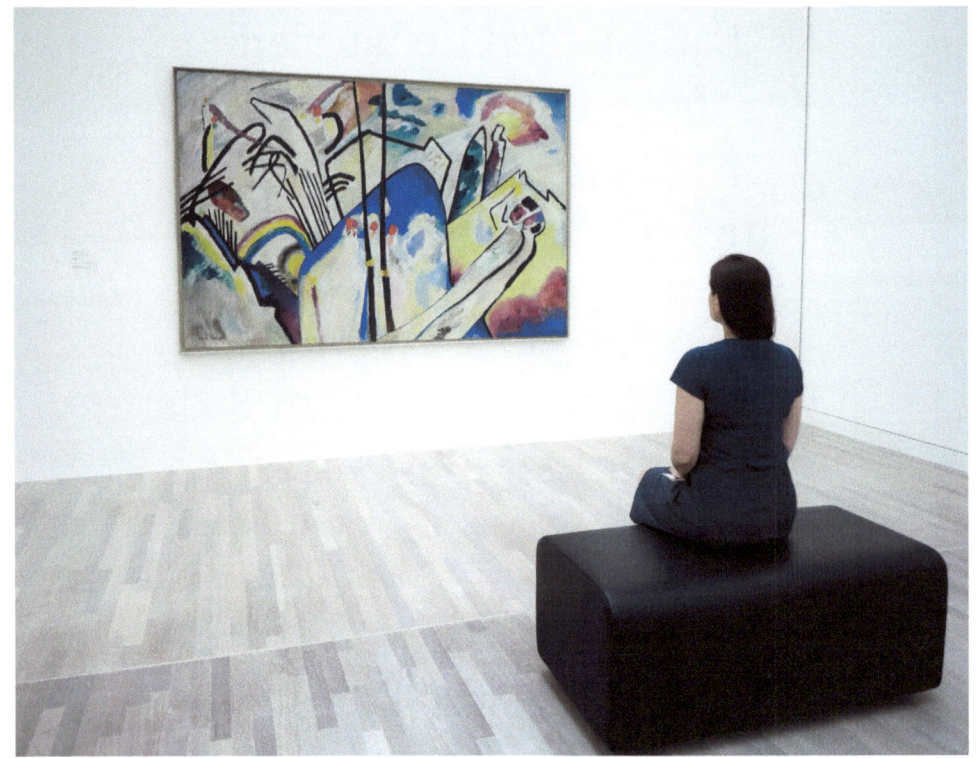

Kandinsky painted leaves
with shades, that others couldn't see.
Red, yellow and blue
were shown with added vibrancy.
He studied Russian folklore
with it's vast variety;
then painted Cossacks, peasants, priests
and all society.

He painted gravestones, houses, trees,
horses, hills and stones.
His colours ever brighter
with louder, bolder tones.

Shapes and forms were simplified,
some hard to recognise.
The manuscript was changing fast
before our very eyes.

Did he hear the striking colours?
Did he see the written score?
Did he feel the faint vibrato?
Did he hear the final roar?

◆ ◆ ◆

Wassily Kandinsky 1866 - 1944

ACKNOWLEDGEMENT

Alamy prints
 FCGK3T BYC136 2B7MJ5K HKN7BC
CRKX4N 2ABTCX9 HGHCC7 TONN8M
W2PHMA D69JBA C62CTC
Sarah Oakey Kirkwood photo of a daisy

ABOUT THE AUTHOR

Lucy Ann Linney

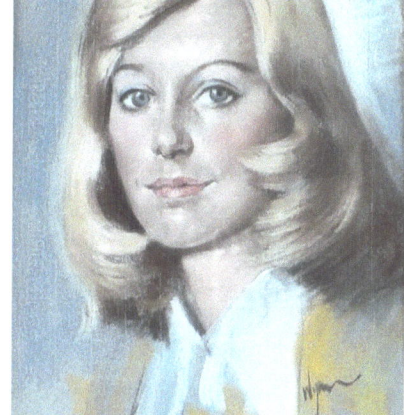

Lucy Ann Linney was born in 1949, the fouth of five children in a very musical family, steeped in church tradition and music.

She grew up surrounded by her brother and her artistic, creative sisters, being in awe of the artwork they produced.

She learnt to play the piano, viola and recorder.

She taught as a primary school teacher, specialising in music.

Married with three children, she remarried in 2012.

In 2018 she discovered that she had developed ovarian cancer. After an operation and chemotherapy treatment, she went back for her all clear appointment, only to be told that there were two more tumours on her lung. Another operation ensued and this time she was given the all clear.

Life is such a precious gift.

Lucy is not one to sit back and dwell on the downside of the last two years, but rather take the opportunity to express herself in a different way.

The next quote seems to be especially poignant.

" Art especially music exists to elevate us as far as possible above everyday existence." Gabriel Faure

BOOKS BY THIS AUTHOR

It's All About The Hat

"Why shouldn't art be pretty? There are enough unpleasant things in the world." Pierre Auguste Renoir.

This is an illustrated book that captures detail in the essence of great paintings.

Everyone sees something different as they contemplate a work of art.

Art can arouse emotions such as joy, love, serenity, peace, anger, melancholy or sadness.

Who could fail to see the beauty in Gustav Klimt's Portrait of Adele Bloch Bauer or see the love in Pierre Auguste Renoir's Luncheon of the Boating Party? Who could fail to feel the nostalgia or pride in J. M. W. Turner's Fighting Temeraire?

In 2020, lockdown has had a huge impact on our lives, often leading to negative feelings. This book could lighten the mood in these unprecedented times.

Sometimes we just want to delve into art and find out a little bit more about the history, the artist or the flavour of the painting.

Through her poetry, Lucy Ann Linney does a little light delving.

www.ingramcontent.com/pod-product-compliance
Lightning Source LLC
Chambersburg PA
CBHW051213220526
45473CB00003B/1017